How To Get There From Here . . . The Ten Lessons That Have Served Me Well

How To Get There From Here . . . The Ten Lessons That Have Served Me Well

Coleman H. Peterson

authorHOUSE®

AuthorHouse™ LLC
1663 Liberty Drive
Bloomington, IN 47403
www.authorhouse.com
Phone: 1-800-839-8640

Published by AuthorHouse   02/06/2014

ISBN: 978-1-4685-3745-1 (sc)
ISBN: 978-1-4685-3744-4 (hc)
ISBN: 978-1-4685-3743-7 (e)

Library of Congress Control Number: 2011963494

Contents

Contents

Foreword

Life is definitely a journey and not just a destination. How could we possibly plot out every detail of a full and purposeful life? How could we even know what the future will bring and how we will fit into that picture? What can we plan and control and what do we need to do to go with the flow? These are questions I am asked as a successful entrepreneur and a community leader. What they are really asking me is, "How did you do it? Can you give me the magic formula? "My answer is almost always a few questions, What is YOUR passion? What do you want to do more than anything else when you wake up every day? What plan are you going to put in place to be sure that your passion becomes your everyday life? How are you going to enjoy all the teachable moments along the way and enhance your personal and professional life?

I was able to turn this curiosity into a successful retail career. I turned every person I met into a mentor—someone I could learn from. I started Build-A-Bear Workshop in 1997 after a successful 20+ year career as a retail executive. Today Build-A-Bear Workshop is a public company traded on the New York Stock Exchange with global revenues over \$400 million.

Cole Peterson is one of my mentors. I have had the advantage of his friendship and coaching for over 25 years. The concepts Cole Peterson introduces within this book—*How to Get There From Here . . . The Ten Lessons That Have served Me Well* is the perfect life planning book for young people starting out in their career or those who want to make a major life or career change. It is never too late to re-think your goals, set a plan and go for it and smell the roses along the way.

How to Get There From Here is a business and life strategy guidebook focused on helping you turn your passion, your personal values into a career that is fulfilling and financially rewarding. It doesn't mean you have to have every detail planned out—quite the opposite—that would take the fun out of life for sure. It would also hinder the mistakes we all must make that keep us humble, help us learn and mature. There are no easy roads to success but *How to Get There From Here* will be an inspiring jump start to your journey.

—Maxine Clark, Founder and CEO, Build-A-Bear Workshop

To: My family,
    My friends and,
    Those unexpected people we meet who stimulate our lives

Introduction

I am a Chicago West Side inner-city kid whose career ultimately took him to a small town in Northwest Arkansas—Bentonville, home of the No. 1 company in *Fortune* magazine's top 500. During my tenure there, Wal-Mart became at times the most reviled, yet the most admired company in the world.

This book is not about Wal-Mart, however. It is about one man's journey from the housing projects of Chicago to a position as the human resource chief of the world's largest private workforce: 1.5 million people. It is a story of my growth during a 32-year career as a corporate human resource executive and how it has shaped my life.

In the course of this book, I hope to share what I have learned in three areas:

- Setting the stage for career building
- Acquiring the essential skill sets
- Clarifying personal values

For whom is this book written? For a number of people. It is written for the person newly entering the workforce, looking to get ahead. It is written for middle managers looking to advance their careers. It is written for the person working for a corporate, governmental or nonprofit organization. Finally, it is written for those who are simply interested in becoming a better person.

Whatever your reason for reading this book, I hope you find what you are seeking.

Blessings,

Cole Peterson

About the Author

Cole Peterson is President/CEO of Hollis Enterprises, LLC, a human resources consulting firm founded in 2004 following his retirement from Wal-Mart Stores, Inc. He specializes in executive coaching and keynote speaking engagements globally.

Peterson, known as America's top people person, served as Executive Vice President of People for Wal-Mart Stores, Inc., where he had the distinction of being the Chief Human Resource Officer of the world's largest private workforce (today: 2.1 million associates worldwide). He headed human resources during Wal-Mart's most aggressive global expansion and helped diversify its workforce. Today, Wal-Mart is the country's No. 1 employer of African Americans and Hispanics.

Peterson serves on the corporate boards of J.B. Hunt Transport of Lowell, Arkansas, Build-A-Bear Workshop of St. Louis, Missouri, and Cracker Barrel Restaurants of Lebanon, Tennessee. He is chairman of the compensation committee on all three boards. He serves on the nominating and corporate governance committees of Build-A-Bear Bear and J.B. Hunt. He is a member of the executive committee and public responsibility committees of Cracker Barrel.

Peterson's numerous recognitions include: The Award for Professional Excellence, The Society for Human Resource Management's highest honor; the Lifetime Achievement Award for Human Resource Excellence from Linkage, Inc.; The Chancellor's Medal for Volunteerism from the University of Arkansas and the Lifetime Achievement Award from the Arkansas MLK Planning Commission. His most recent recognitions are the National Association of African Americans in Human Resource Professionals Trail Blazer Award and the Lifetime Achievement Award from the Arkansas Society for Human Resource Management State Council. Peterson is a Fellow of the Academy of Human Resources, and a member of both Kappa Alpha Psi and Sigma Pi Phi fraternities.

Peterson is a native of Birmingham, Alabama, and grew up in Chicago where he obtained his bachelor's and master's degrees from Loyola University. He and his wife, Shirley, have two adult children and reside in Hilton Head Island, South Carolina.

Lesson 1

Have a Goal

We're off to see the Wizard . . .
—Dorothy

How often have you heard the saying, "If you don't know where you are going, any road will get you there"? It is so true. When you aim or strive for something, you know at least that your personal drive should move you in that direction; so if you do not hit the mark, at least you will be in the neighborhood! Dorothy found herself in an environment where she was not familiar, without friends and without experience. Yet, her outcome was successful. Why? Because, she developed a goal: follow the yellow brick road to see the wizard! As motivational speaker Les Brown says, "Shoot for the moon. Even if you miss, you will land among the stars."

Growing up in the inner city of Chicago, my favorite time of year was around the Christmas holidays. My mother would always take my older brother and me downtown to see the Christmas lights and all of the department store windows beautifully decorated with their colorful winter scenes. We would stand on our tiptoes and press our noses against the windows, amazed at the beauty and excitement of it all.

At about age 9 or 10, I remember noticing all of the business people making their way through the crowds. They were sharply dressed in suits, overcoats, and hats, with the ever-present briefcase clutched in one hand. They always appeared important and self-assured, but in a hurry. I was fascinated by them. Even though I had no idea who they were or what they did, I told my mother, "Mama, I'm gonna do that one day." "That's good, baby," she would say.

Twenty years later, while heading up the executive recruiting function for one of the retail divisions of the May Department Stores Company (now Macy's), I flew into Nashville, Tennessee, late one night. I was pretty preoccupied as I deplaned and walked briskly through the airport. As I exited the terminal, I saw a young boy being tugged along by his mother as he pointed at me and said, "See, Mama, that's what I want to be when I grow up!" I was startled out of my own thoughts, back into reality; he was talking about me. As I turned to wave and smile at him, I caught my reflection in the airport glass: I was rather nicely dressed in my business suit, overcoat, hat—with my ever-present briefcase in hand. The power of imagining and goal setting had come full circle.

So what exactly is the difference between "goal setting" and "pipe dreaming"? You have had situations where a friend or acquaintance has shared his or her plan for the future, and you sympathetically rolled your eyes and thought to yourself, "Get a life and a real job, pal, 'cause *this* ain't gonna happen!"

My own view is that dreaming is helpful in goal setting. Any vision or picture of the future that motivates you and causes you to put one foot in front of the other in pursuit of that objective is a good thing. After all, how many people do you know who are aimless? They are going through life going through the motions, without enthusiasm or joy about its possibilities. Which way would you choose to move through life?

Dreams are a wild fancy or hope. They are also a target at which you can aim. However, dreams can be as big as you want them to be. Dreams can have an indefinite or clear-cut timetable for fulfillment. Dreams are your eventual targets; goals are mileposts that mark the way. Dreams are what you ultimately want and goals get you to those dreams. Dreams do not have to be outlined as specifically as a goal. Goals require more effort to achieve. To achieve any goal, you have to want to change more than you want to stay the same.

Over the years, in both my professional human resource career and my personal life, I have had occasions to coach and counsel people about goal setting. I never try to discourage dreams; rather, I approach making dreams come true by translating them into *actionable behaviors*—these become goals. For example, many people's favorite goal is financial success: "I want to make $100,000 by the time I am 30 years old." This is fine; however, the question becomes, "How do I get there from here?" It will require specific actions that may not appear to be that grandiose. For example, finishing high school would be a good start (goal one), finishing college would be another good step (goal two), and acquiring a good entry-level job after college would be great (goal three). I would add that the major you pursue in college could influence how quickly you reach your long-term goal after college. The physician is much more likely to make those kinds of dollars than a social worker or teacher! Yet, if your goal is to change lives in an entirely different way, the social worker and the teacher are clearly special in their contributions. Once you begin employment, you then set both occupational and financial goals. So, what others might see as 'pipe dreams' are simply your long-term goals. Every dream begins with the first step.

How will you know when you have achieved your dream? Goal setting is knowing where you want to go and setting up a plan for getting there. When you know where you want to go in life, then you know where to put your efforts. Because your focus should be single-minded toward your goals, you will be able to see distractions very quickly. Seeing distractions is good, because this will compel you to get back on track and refocus. Therefore, goal setting is a great thing; however, make sure your goals are *attainable, motivating,* and *specific.*

Let's examine how this looks in black-and-white. For instance, you say that you want to lose 25 pounds, be healthy, and have a sleek physique. The goal is the marker along the way to the dream. You have to set specific steps. For example:

- Start an exercise program of working out at least three days a week.
- Cut down on your carbohydrate intake.
- Drink more water.
- Eat more fruits and vegetables.

These steps take your dream from being a dream to a goal. Then, you can even take your goal to the next level by specifying which days of the week you will work out, for how long each day, which carbohydrates you will cut back on, and even how much water you will drink each day. Once again, goals help you become more focused.

It is good to evaluate your goals every so often to see if you are still on target. Also, keep in mind that you can tweak your goals if they are not working for you. For example, if cutting your carbohydrate intake is not working, you could do some research to determine the best carbohydrates to cut from your diet and which ones are okay to continue. Keep in mind that goals are guideposts on the journey and not the destination itself.

> What you get by achieving your goals is not as important
> as what you become by achieving your goals.
> —Zig Ziglar

It is amazing to consider what we have become as we look back through our lives. Consider the importance of this young boy's childhood, and how it may have affected who he became: The four-year-old sat in the hall and watched his mother cry. Her body went limp like a rag doll. Behind her, the Christmas tree sparkled. That year changed the memory of Christmas forever in Tim Broughton's mind. Each season, as December approached, his blood stirred with anxiety. Others were buoyant during the holidays, shopping and caroling and celebrating, but Tim felt sickened. The time was associated with the most traumatic event in his life: the day his father walked out and disappeared forever.

I first heard Tim speak at a Champions for Kids "Salute to the Stars" fundraiser in Northwest Arkansas. It was a magnificent event, sponsored by companies like Walt Disney and ABC, and Tim, who was the vice president of the billion-dollar corporation, McKee Foods, stood before the crowded auditorium, his face stoic and brave, a grown man choking back tears.

I sat in the audience with other business leaders, and a knot formed in my throat. It was December 13—almost 44 years to the day—since Tim's dad had left. Tim told how his father cleared the bank accounts, and how his mother, an alcoholic, tried her best to raise the children. What does all this have to do with goals?

As much as you would like to think you have the power to shape your own life, you also are shaped by life and the people and experiences you encounter. Tim's story exemplified how both the good and the bad in life make you who you are and mold you into the individual you will become. It was hard to sit and listen to Tim tell his story, and as he choked to get through it, his words took me back to my own beginnings. He talked about the night he and his sisters huddled in a blanket on the couch, in a cold house with no food, and how he will remember forever the hunger pangs of that one moment. Tim talked about the basketball coach in high school, who called him into the office quietly to give him sneakers, so as not to embarrass him in front of his teammates. He told the crowd about people who had helped him and his family along the way, and how he remembered the kindness more than anything else. Tim's speech reminded me that every encounter might bring a person who needs a hand up because everybody has a goal and a dream.

As I sat there and listened, I reflected on the turning points in my own life, like the time I flew into Chicago, the city where I had grown up, but I flew there in a corporate jet. Later that same day, I drove a rental car through the drug-infested, broken-down projects that could have held me back. That singular moment made me see how far I had come. I had a goal, and I worked to achieve it. But the night I heard Tim speak, I knew that even if some of us have worked to leave our past behind, it is there for a reason. Your past isn't irrelevant. The mistakes, the successes, and the hurts all comprise the mosaic of who you are now. Those early experiences help form and define who we are and who we will become.

How is it that some people rise from the ashes of broken lives and the sands of mediocrity to achieve great things? This question continues to fascinate and awe. News broadcasts show rags-to-riches stories about people who were abused, abandoned, or raised in abject poverty and went on to become CEOs, billionaires, and world leaders. It is a question that fascinated me as a human resource professional who witnessed an endless and diverse stream of people walking through my door. Despite the darkest of backgrounds, some just shined—their victory and belief in themselves clearly visible, like an Eagle Scout badge on their lapel. Others, sadly, did not shine as brightly. It was evident that some people were being held back by their own limiting beliefs and goals.

Tim Broughton stepped up and realized his goal, even though the odds were stacked against him early on. Life got much worse after his father left; his mother remarried, to a child molester and abuser, he reports. Despite how he grew up, Tim earned a full scholarship to college, got a 3.51 GPA, and majored in applied mathematics. He was accepted into an officer training program in the military and finished second in the entire class! By the time I met him, he was the vice president of a billion-dollar corporation. He had a goal and a dream, and he worked to make it happen.

It's the human encounters you have and the way you interact with others that shape the world. Those experiences, depending on how you interpret them and react to them, will determine how far you can go. They define what kind of person you are and into what kind of person you will evolve.

Have a goal and dream big!

> Setting goals is the first step in turning
> the invisible into the visible.
> —Anthony Robbins

Lesson 2

No Shortcuts

Judge a man, not by the heights he achieves, but from the depths from which he has risen.
—Frederick Douglass

I really enjoyed late-night TV talk shows like *The Tonight Show, Starring Johnny Carson* or today's version with Jay Leno. Interviews with film stars and celebrities always have been of particular interest to me. The celebrities were always so cool and glamorous, and the audiences would go crazy, heaping loud applause and admiration. I'm sure that among the admirers were those who wanted to be "just like them."

As the nighttime host would speak glowingly of the guest star's screen roles and award nominations, I always waited patiently to hear the all-important question, "How did you get started?" The answers always were fascinating. Many of the stars began their careers waiting tables and working in retail stores while waiting for their big break. Commercials and bit parts for years preceded stardom for many men and women. It is a great message: no shortcuts.

Early in my career, I spent several years as a college recruiter for my company. I always was fascinated by graduating seniors who had no sense of beginning on the bottom rung of the corporate ladder. Furthermore, once many of them entered the world of work, they complained that they were relegated to menial tasks and "were not learning anything."

In truth, when most of us start in life, there is very little that we *do* know—the rest of life is filling the gaps. We have heard many stories of a dad lecturing his child about how to do chores: "Anything worth doing is worth doing well."

As a part of the feedback I sought from new college hires, I always enjoyed getting their progress reports at six, 12, and 18 months. With few exceptions, the new hires felt that they were not moving fast enough. They thought that they knew everything there was to know and that they were prepared to move to the next challenge.

For human resource professionals and career-path specialists, this is always a tricky call: balancing the impatience of talent that shows potential, with the need to ensure that they have the required skills to succeed. I understand this intimately because of my own early experience. After graduating from college, I began working in a retail training program in Chicago. Upon starting in the program, while I was at my first training store, I encountered three management trainees who immediately informed me of the terrible mistake I had made by coming to the company, and—by the way—they were all planning to quit Friday!

Considering that I was rather low on funds (broke, to be more accurate!), I decided to stick it out. I also felt that I had an ace in the hole. My dear fraternity brother was a hiring manager at one of the big-time insurance companies downtown. I figured I would go down there and give him the old fraternity handshake and catapult myself into a new white-collar career, equipped with business cards, an office, and a company car. What I discovered that day has formed the basis for my own approach to success as well as the counsel that I offer others.

Bob Corbett explained that I had been with my current company for barely three months. He refused to even consider me for his company before I had committed at least one year with the other company! He was quite explicit and explained, "Not 11 months and 29 days, but one year on the job!"

Needless to say, I was sorely disappointed—crushed. With no real options, I returned to my job, determined to work hard, tough it out, and reapply with my friend in 12 months and one day. That day never came.

As I began to apply myself to the job, I discovered that there was a lot to learn about merchandising, transportation, finance, and—most of all—managing people. I discovered that through people that I had a knack for getting things done, and I enjoyed hiring, training, and developing people. I did well; in fact, I did quite well. By the end of year one, I had been promoted three times, and by the end of year two, I was promoted to the home office, to a new role that became my career profession: human resources.

I had several conversations with Bob Corbett subsequent to that initial chat, thanking him for his sound advice. He obviously knew then what I later learned: success occurs over time—there are no shortcuts.

Champions know there are no shortcuts to the top.
They climb the mountain one step at a time.
They have no use for helicopters.
—Judi Adler (Author)

Are you starting to see things differently? Human resources executives see the things business leaders generally can't see, either because they're not looking hard enough, they don't have the time, or they don't have the desire to know anything more than what "results" an employee can offer their business. In your own organization, how do you see your people? What is it that the leaders at the highest levels think about their employees? How well you can see will determine how well you manage, and how you manage will influence your success.

When interviewing an internal candidate for a promotion or an external candidate for a new position, I always read his or her résumé backward. I go to the last page of the résumé (the candidate's beginnings) and read it forward to the present (the candidate's current status), because this method offers insight into where a person began. I know that the shortcut would be to go directly to the heart of what he or she is doing and skip the rest, but wisdom has taught me that is not the thing to do.

Reading a résumé backward allows you to understand how far someone has come and how hard he or she has worked to get there. It reveals a lot. In the end, it's all about growth. How has he grown? Has she had a desire to grow? Did the person take shortcuts or do it the old-fashioned way?

These are important questions, not just for a potential employee, but for you to ask yourself as well. How have you grown? How do you want to grow and what are the steps that you need to take? It is the same process you should follow when you evaluate prospective employees and where their occupational journeys have taken them. The *what* is just as important to evaluate as the *where* and the *why* of an individual's professional history. What has he or she done? Is it different, broader, or better than what the individual did before?

There is a distinction between five years' experience and one year of experience multiplied five times. A person can perform a role in an organization and not have any greater understanding, skill, or ability after having been in that role five years as he or she did after the first year. This isn't growth; it's stagnation. One would hope after five years in a job that there is an accumulation of various exposures, skill development and experiences. To only have "one year's experience five times" means that one has not had any new learnings or practices beyond the first 12 months in the position.

You can determine a lot by asking a prospective hire: "How have you grown?" This open-ended question should reveal a lot about the person and his or her willingness and desire to grow. It will also tell you how he or she might help develop and add value to a team, department, or company. Don't ignore the answer. I can recall watching in admiration as a defense attorney handled the cross-examination of a witness, in two separate courtroom situations, two years apart. I observed her in one year and again about two years later. The difference was amazing. Initially, although quite capable, she was tentative and somewhat unsure of herself. Later, she was firm, confident and quite savvy in the courtroom! It was obvious that as a function of her practice and real-time exposure she had grown noticeably. I compare this with an attorney friend of mine who has been in the profession for quite a few years now, but does not appear to have acquired a level of experience, approach and know-how that should be consistent with his time in the profession.

Organizations are a slice of real life. Whatever takes place in the real world always will be duplicated to some degree in your organization. When I was asked to give a speech at Yale, I titled it "Culture and Stuff," to demonstrate the simplistic way we communicated and defined our company culture at Wal-Mart. Wal-Mart's first of three company values: "Respect for

22

the Individual." I talked about our company motto: "Hire for attitude, train for skill." When I presented this speech again, it was in El Salvador. The audience was very different, but the message was the same. No matter what kind of organization you are a part of, if your strategy is focused on people, the message that a company's interest in treating people well, having employees grow and succeed, transcends all boundaries and cultural differences. There are no shortcuts for focusing on the needs of people.

Most companies focus on short-term results that can get them to the numbers quickly, which means implementing a quick turnaround strategy, restructuring, or including a new consultant-driven program. It is like trying to get a tree sapling to grow in a particular direction by holding it in place, rather than using stakes and a rope to stabilize it and train its growth naturally in the desired direction. Companies that ratchet down on expenses to generate a needed profit in one fiscal year can damage equipment, relationships and people who make it impossible for the company to sustain the same results over time. A strategy for generational growth will reflect a balance on requiring results while developing a "ground up" understanding by the organization of why we are doing what we are doing. Sometimes these solutions are effective, but they are short-term solutions, not strategies for generational growth.

Just as there are no shortcuts to good health, there are no shortcuts to success. For instance, right after New Year's Day, gyms are packed with people who want to lose weight. They work out for a few weeks and they do so with good intentions; however, by the time February rolls around they revert to old habits: overeating and not getting enough exercise. They tried to take a shortcut—work out really hard for just a few weeks—then, after they didn't see the desired results, they soon slipped into their old ways. Balance, moderation, and consistency create change. It is no different with success in any area of your life. If you want to be successful, you must work at it. Avoid shortcuts. It is unrealistic to come into a company straight out of college and be the CEO. Now, that could happen, but the likelihood is very slim! However, if you join with a company, dig your heels in, and work hard, the possibility of rising to the position of CEO becomes more realistic. Don't be afraid of working hard, being patient, and climbing the ladder of success, rung by rung, to the top.

There are no shortcuts to any place worth going.
—Beverly Sills (Opera Singer)

Lesson 3

Work Hard

All the so-called "secrets of success"
will not work unless you do.
—Author Unknown

Tiger Woods is an athlete whose professional accomplishments amazed us all. I never played much golf until I retired a few years ago. I was looking forward to finally driving my triple-digit score down into the mid-eighties. Some years later, I am fighting to keep a 21 handicap! Equipped with cutting-edge golf technology and attired in the latest Nike duds, I head to the first tee and wonder why my drive barely makes it beyond the women's tee box. Could it be because I don't practice?

Tiger's high school golf coach wrote a book about Tiger and his early success at the game of golf. Don Crosby's book, *Tiger Woods Made Me Look Like a Genius* focused primarily on Tiger's approach to the game, rather than what Crosby taught him as his coach. Crosby observed that every aspect of the game seemed to be a practice exercise for Tiger. He explained how Tiger would play a round of golf, but in the process, he might play the approach shot to a certain hole several different times, in several different ways. For example, he would practice an approach shot out of the nearby rough, then a chip shot from the fairway and he would work the fairway and the green so often and so many ways that what looked like magic to us was merely an execution of what he knew would happen because he had done it many, many times. That takes hard work.

Some may wonder why I chose Tiger Woods as an example of hard work, in light of the recent challenges in his personal life. It was of such note that I conferred with others to gain a broader perspective. The fact remains that Tiger's accomplishments are truly singular in many ways. It is impossible to discount the discipline and hard work that his dad instilled in him as a boy and how well that has served him in his professional career.

To this point, perhaps it is fair to say that we will see if the hard work that made Tiger Woods the No. 1 golfer in the world for 281 consecutive weeks (June 12, 2005 through October 24, 2010) will assist him in returning to that status.

> Dictionary is the only place that success comes before
> work. Hard work is the price we must pay for success.
> I think you can accomplish anything if you're
> willing to pay the price.
> —Vince Lombardi

What is your attitude toward work? Much has been written about the good old American work ethic, how the West was won by men and women who conquered hostile environments to make their way forward by the sweat of their brows and the strength of their backs. The early American landscape was filled with the work product of steel mills, automotive manufacturing plants, and mining operations. That work was hard and dangerous. Others toiled on farms, where they raised crops, and nursed livestock, all to feed their families. As we look back at how these times are depicted, they seem to be underscored with the message of how hard one has to work. Do we get that sense today? We have moved from a manufacturing-based economy to a service-oriented economy; does that transition carry with it a reality that we are not willing to work as hard?

The Boston Globe published an article on February 20, 2006[1], revealing that the U.S. military was relaxing its basic training standards for new recruits. The admission standards had been lowered because the U.S. Army faced greater difficulty in meeting recruiting goals and a number of potential recruits were unable to pass the basic requirements. The requirement changes included revising tests to accommodate overweight candidates. This came on the heels of reports that teenage obesity has climbed from 5 percent to 16 percent over the last 30 years (The Centers for Disease Control and Prevention reports that as of September 15, 2011, adolescents aged 12-19 years who were obese increased from 5 percent to 18 percent in this same period). Other changes incorporated included helping potential recruits acquire GEDs (a good thing) and reducing the time to reapply from 180 days to 45 days if a recruit tested positive for marijuana.

What is the significance of this? I believe it is an indictment upon us that we continue to lower our standards to meet the situation. This relaxation of standards certainly addresses a practical problem; however, where do we land over time? As we shape our own plans for the future, exactly how hard are we willing to work? Do we see role models encourage and challenge our work ethic? Do we believe that hard work will yield positive, winning results?

My own take on this is mixed. I have worked with and counseled those whose objectives are to get as much as possible by doing as little as possible. I am never sure whether the person across the desk from me has given 100 percent, or whether he or she simply discourages easily. Our drive, after all, can come from two places: internal and external.

We tend to focus a great deal on how we are driven by others: a demanding CEO, a tough, hard-charging football coach, an Army drill sergeant, or even a demanding parent. These external players truly can drive us to a level of performance that, on our own, we might not have attained. This is a good thing. We have often seen how the relentless coach can help players push beyond their own original boundaries to reach personal bests. In our career journey, we may experience several external forces that can act upon us whether we want them to or not. Or, we can invite this driving force into our lives as an aide or helper, such as a personal coach or mentor. This outward driving force can produce positive results.

The inner drive is the intangible, spiritual aspect of working hard. It is the element that causes us to rise early and stay up late. It is the invisible driver that demands that we redo our presentation many times, even though it already is good. It is the intangible that drives us to be as good as we possibly can-not because someone expects it, but because we expect it.

I witnessed this force at work in the past, when I visited with my son and daughter, who were watching a Texas high school playoff game in which the score was already 41-10 in the third quarter. I commented on how impressive the team was, when both kids said, "Watch this dad." Sure enough, on the next play, the tall, thin quarterback for the leading team ran through the line and scampered toward the goal line as three defenders piled on, and he dragged them toward the end zone! It was amazing to watch. There is no doubt that the young quarterback had been taught a lot of techniques and plays by his coach. He also certainly was driven and challenged to be better by his coach. Yet as I watched this young man press toward the goal line, it was clear that he had an inner drive that raised his performance to another level.

So far in this chapter I might have emphasized the importance of working hard to the point that I possibly have failed to note that working smart is certainly important. I believe that those who give the greatest effort always will win. Effort does, however, need to be coupled with taking advantage of everything at your disposal—education, supervisory feedback, and mentoring, for example.

This is illustrated in the story of three men who were fishing offshore. The first fisherman said to the other two that he could walk on water back to land. "No way," said the third, whereupon the first fisherman stepped out of the boat and miraculously walked on water back to the shore. In shock, the third fisherman said, "How did he do that?" The second fisherman, unimpressed, then threw down his rod, hopped out of the boat, and walked on the water, back to the shore. The third fisherman, a real competitor, not to be outdone, looked at the two men waving from the shore, took a deep breath, climbed overboard and immediately began to sink. Fortunately, he resurfaced and climbed, soaking wet, back into the boat. The first fisherman looked at the second fisherman and said, "Do you think we should tell him where the rocks are?"

We all can use a little help to make our hard work pay off.

If you look back a few generations, you will see that your ancestors really knew what hard work was all about. It was routine for them to rise early in the morning, before sunrise. They often would work from sun up to sundown. Many worked in factories. However, before they got to the factory, they had fed the cows and horses and maybe even worked in the garden. In order for people to feed their families, they were required to do much manual labor. They knew how to use their hands before machines came along. Hats off to them!

> Opportunity is missed by most people because it is dressed
> in overalls and looks like work.
> —Thomas Edison

The days of our ancestors' type of work are gone. Yes, we still use our hands to work but in a much different way. Many of us don't have to use our bodies for physical labor when it comes to working. You might say, "I work out at the gym," and that is great. Many people sit at a desk for most of their workday. Life can be very stationary. You might perform some physical labor, but our forefathers had none of the modern conveniences that we enjoy.

You may be saying now, "Hey, I work from sun up to sundown!" Is working long hours the same as working hard? It can be. It just depends. For some, working long hours means watching a machine do all of the work for an eight-hour shift. For others, working long hours means loading heavy packages or equipment onto an assembly line. We might differ in our opinions regarding the similarities between working long and working hard. I believe that, depending upon the worker, the two can be one in the same. Once again, if you look at the past, those who harvested crops and often were paid by the amount of produce they picked, certainly had to spend more time in the fields if they wanted to make more money. I would say that they worked both long and hard.

If your goal in life is to make it to the next level, then pushing yourself is required. No matter where you are in life, you must have drive, motivation, and be willing to work hard if you want to be successful. That goes for all jobs.

As I'm writing this book, I feel as though I'm working hard because I'm having to use my mental capacities. There are those who might disagree with me; however, mental jobs can be just as taxing as physical ones. It must be very demanding, hard work to be a brain surgeon, a nuclear physicist, or any other highly skilled position. Therefore, a case can be made that mental labor as well as physical labor are examples of hard work.

Even with mental exertion, how hard are we willing to work these days? I submit that even our technologies have created a mental laziness. We are living in the age of technology. You can have just about everything right at your fingertips. There are BlackBerries, i-Phones, GPS systems, the Internet, Twitter and the list continues. Our work has been made a lot easier because we can get access to so much information in a matter of seconds. In some ways this can benefit us; in others it might not. Because we are able to get information so quickly, we learn to expect fast service in everything. This can lead to frustration, for example, when you might have to wait in line at a restaurant for 15 minutes; that seems just too long when you are used to getting things in a nanosecond.

It took Thomas Edison approximately 14 months to develop a practical light bulb. That task took a lot of mental and physical energy without the benefit of modern conveniences. He worked long and he worked hard.

The difference between try and triumph is a little umph.
—Author Unknown

One of the best examples of working hard that I have seen is in my own household. My son, Collin, had just completed his senior year of high school and was preparing to move on to college in the fall. For two summers he had worked for a local entrepreneur who ran a packing and shipping center. His boss, Bill, was quite demanding, and, of course, quite protective of the business that he had worked so hard to build. Bill worked six days a week, every day that the business is open. One day, my son came home and said "Guess what, Bill is taking tomorrow [Saturday] off, and he put me in charge!" I was surprised and impressed at this. We often use the term "giving someone the keys to the store," and here it was literally happening to my own son. I explained to him what a big deal this was. I emphasized that the rewards for hard work are additional responsibility and additional opportunity. I explained that hard work is often recognized and appreciated, even when we think others are not noticing.

Above all, make sure that you work hard. Ask yourself, "Am I working hard or hardly working?" Hardly working is a running joke in many areas, but yet it takes place in so many organizations. Whether you own your business or work for someone else, work hard! The benefits of hard work eventually will pay off and get you where you want to go. Sometimes you have to take risks to achieve goals. Along with risks come fears, but you must be willing to work beyond whatever fears you have. Weigh the odds and see what you have to lose, or better yet, what you have to gain. Those who achieved success were willing to press beyond their fears. You can be anything that you want to be if you are willing to work hard. Are you the master of your fate? Go for it!

Apply yourself. Get all the education you can, but then,
by God, do something. Don't just stand there,
make it happen.
—Lee Iacocca

Lesson 4

Education is an Opportunity
and a Privilege

I hear, and I forget. I see, and I remember.
I do, and I understand.
—Chinese Proverb

In 2003, I was appointed to the board of trustees of NorthWest Arkansas Community College, a fairly new, cutting-edge, and growing college established to meet the expanding needs of the business community in the region. As a part of our trustee role, the board attends the annual graduation exercises. At my first official ceremony, seated on the stage, I could see the various robed graduates, seated according to major and specialty, preparing to receive their associate's degrees. The largest section by far was a group that was quite animated and excited. They were taking pictures, waving at friends and family, and just having an all-around good time.

Curious about their area of degree specialty, I leaned over to one of the senior trustees and asked her. She smiled and said, "Oh, those are the students who just completed their GEDs. My first reaction was to ask myself what, in the lives of each of these individuals (most of whom were quite young), had caused them to leave the traditional education system?

As an individual who has had the opportunity to travel the globe observing business practices and education worldwide, I have seen that the lack of educational opportunities (and the consequences of this deficit) in parts of Africa, South America, Latin America, and Asia are apparent—and they are crippling. Living in a country like America, where a high school education is free and expected, it seemed hard to understand why these young people had dropped out of high school in the first place. Education can be such an equalizer; why would one miss any opportunity to build that strong foundation that is so necessary? And then I realized the answer.

I realized, sitting there watching all of these young people celebrating this milestone, that everyone had a story to tell, and that each story is filled with personal challenges, miscues, and tragedies that could befall us all. As I looked at the faces of the eager GED recipients, I realized that this was truly a day of celebration. Whatever the obstacles were that had impeded these graduates' "regular" movement through the educational system, they had achieved that critical first level that offers access to the job market. So, as each one walked across the stage, I wanted to stand up and give them a high five. I also had no doubt that many of them would go on to complete additional education. Whatever held them back initially was now motivating them into the future. They saw education as an opportunity and a privilege. As the saying goes, hindsight is 20/20.

We each can travel such different educational paths. Oftentimes that path can begin as early as our grammar school days. As I look back on my pre-high school education, I can see that I was never aware that I was the product of an inner-city school. Today, we hear about how sub-standard these schools can be. Fortunately that was not my experience in my early education. I learned from dedicated, sharing teachers who found joy in watching us grow. I remember my third- and sixth-grade teachers, Mrs. Jones and Mr. Mock. They both had a profound impact on my attitude toward education.

Mrs. Jones's impact wasn't a result of what she taught me as much as a result of the warm, safe, and loving environment within her third-grade classroom. At such a young age, I wanted to come to school to receive her infectious smile and loving hugs. It was a wonderful place to be. My experience was even topped off with milk and cookies every day at noon! Within that third-grade bubble, my classmates and I were free to explore and grow as we were exposed to new things.

Mr. Mock taught me the power of the written word. In his sixth-grade class, he read aloud to us and had us take turns reading aloud to one another. He once read the poem *Casey at the Bat* and had us all sitting on the edge of our seats. (I still cannot believe that Casey struck out!) Mr. Mock showed a classroom of inner-city kids that there was a broad, exciting world out there. If that world could not be visited personally, it could be reached through literature that allowed one to go twenty thousand leagues under the sea or float down the Mississippi River with Tom Sawyer and Huckleberry Finn.

> The whole world opened to me when I learned to read.
> —Mary McLeod Bethune

Is education a privilege? In my family, and the black community, (although I believe this is true in all working class and new immigrant communities), it is believed that education was the way up and out. It was clear that the way to have a chance to make a good living "by the sweat of our brow and not just our back," I had to prepare myself through a higher level of education. Access to white-collar, managerial and professional employment expects higher educational attainment. While you might not think of education as an opportunity and privilege because it has always been a part of your life, just look at other parts of the world and it won't take you long to answer this question with a resounding "yes." Education is indeed a privilege.

If we look at schooling in some parts of Africa or in third-world countries, we see that education takes on a different identity. Girls are not at the top of the list to be educated. Do they consider education an opportunity and privilege? No doubt.

While sitting in an airport lounge right after New Year's Day 2007, I watched a clip of Oprah Winfrey on the screen as she announced her $40-million contribution to establish a school for girls in South Africa. Oprah had already been quite involved in education in the United States, according to the report, but many questioned why she would choose to go to South Africa. Oprah explained, "If you ask the kids [in the United States], what they want or need, they will say an iPod or some sneakers. In South Africa, they don't ask for money or toys. They ask for uniforms so they can go to school."

When you look at a country like China, which has a literacy rate of 96.1 percent[2], you will see that education is considered an opportunity and privilege. China boasts some of the highest test scores in the world in math and science. China places a high value on education, and this shows in the high performance of the students there. Public education is compulsory. Do the students consider education an opportunity and privilege? What do you think?

In middle-to upper-class America, we have so many things at our fingertips that it is easy to become desensitized to problems in other parts of the world and even at our own back door. In our society, education is the norm. It can be hard for us to understand why everyone in the world does not have a high school education or college degree.

> The beautiful thing about learning is that no one can take
> it **away** from you.
> —B.B. King

Only about 28 percent of adults in the United States over age 25 have a college degree. That is approximately one in five. If you can afford to get an education at that level, you are ahead of 70 percent of the population.[3] There are many who cannot afford to go to college, just as there are some in other countries who cannot even attend public schools. Even in countries where public schools are free, armed conflict can cause it to be too dangerous for children to attend school.[4]

Public schools in the United States are quite different from one state to the next and even from one city to the next. According to a news report on *Good Morning America*[5], it is not unheard of for students to walk into their classrooms in New York City, smoking marijuana. Also in a New York City school[6], there was a teacher who was not fired for sending a 16-year-old student e-mails that contained sexual content. It took six years for the litigation to make its way through the courts before the teacher finally could be fired. In the same news report, there was a conversation about a student who had attended a public school in South Carolina for 12 years and still could not read a single sentence at the first-grade level. These are tragedies, to say the least.

For African Americans, education is certainly an opportunity and a privilege. Many of our ancestors fought long and hard and even lost their lives so that we could get an education. In the history of the slave trade in America, we know that for slaves to even learn to read without losing their lives was a frightening risk as well as a precious opportunity. Being able to set foot in a school was a dream come true for many African Americans. Still wondering if your educational opportunities are a privilege? American slaves would have said absolutely! It is all about perspective.

If you are part of a family that values education and is willing to make the necessary sacrifices to see that you get a good education, be sure to tell them how much you appreciate their doing that for you. You are fortunate because this is not the norm for many people living in this world today. Many individuals have to work to put themselves through school. There are many who put their education off until after they started their career and then decide to go to college. Therefore, they are working a 40-hour job and getting an education at the same time. To the person who has to work and go to school, education is an opportunity and privilege. Also, let us not forget the single parent who is working to make ends meet while going to school. They know, without any doubt, that education is an opportunity and privilege.

I know that for me personally, education has been an opportunity and a privilege. The way that I was nurtured from grade school through college by various teachers along the way was part of what helped me to get to where I am in life today.

> There is a brilliant child locked inside every student.
> —Marva Collins

I would be remiss if I said that all education takes place in a formal classroom setting. Because of technology, education can take place in the comfort of your own home. It is entirely possible to get a college degree, from bachelor's to Ph.D., right in your own house. Additionally, there are all kinds of technical institutes that offer classes. We certainly can't forget about those who are homeschooled, either.

For some people, skills are equally as important as a formal education. We have seen many people who have become successful even though they did not get a four-year college degree. Bill Gates is one of those individuals. He is one of the richest men in the world. His story is very interesting because he did not finish college. He dropped out of Harvard in his junior year to get his world-renowned company, Microsoft, going. Entrepreneur, H. Ross Perot, attended junior college but did not continue his education at a university. Instead he became the billionaire founder of Electronic Data Systems. Arguably the most profound impact player of our time was Steve Jobs—inventor, entrepreneur and co-founder of Apple, Inc., Jobs completed one semester of college as he forged his incredible career. These men serve as prime examples of people who have demonstrated that education is important, but the ability to couple education with skills is the key.

You have to make the decision based on your life, circumstances, and experiences as to whether you will consider education to be an opportunity and a privilege.

Intelligence plus character—that is the goal of true education.
—Martin Luther King, Jr.

Lesson 5

Listen: Understand the Power of Feedback

I know that you believe you understand what you think
I said, but I'm not sure you realize that what
you heard is not what I meant.
—Robert McCloskey (Author)

The story of the three elderly women taking a train ride into the countryside is one of my favorites. As the train is rattling along, the first woman comments, "My, it's windy." The second responds, "No, it is not Wednesday, it is Thursday," whereupon the third woman exclaims, "Yes, I am thirsty too! Let's all get off at the next stop and have a nice cup of tea." The capacity to listen is linked so strongly to our ability to hear and process feedback, to absorb the way others see us, in order to improve how we behave, act, and relate to others.

A key characteristic of those who succeed and achieve their life and career goals is having the ability to understand the power of feedback. Not everyone understands the academic, psychological underpinnings of how listening works, yet some have mastered it as a part of improving themselves.

When we were younger, our parents liked to describe us as "hard-headed." In other words, we did not listen. And of course, when we reached the teen years, there was nothing that an adult could share that would possibly be of any value. Remember how your kids explained to you how much smarter *you* became when *they* reached their mid-20s? Feedback, by its very nature, is not an easy or natural process. Listening can be difficult because feedback, for most of us, means criticism that comes after we make a mess of something. We will discuss this later, but this comes from a lack of balance in the feedback we receive—not all feedback is or should be negative.

Feedback occurs from the time we are out of the womb—the first responses from our parents, who applaud us as we learn our first words or learn to take our first steps, or who teach us the sound of the word "No!" which is designed to protect us from something harmful and which begins to shape how we understand the rules of acceptable social behavior.

As a senior human resource executive, I had to referee many performance disputes at the highest levels. This, of course, is where an executive who earns $200,000 a year is failing to perform in the eyes of his superior, and the facts must be sorted to determine what is one individual's perception and what is reality.

Generally, the higher up the organizational ladder one climbs, the more difficult it is to accept feedback unless one has developed this skill early. Three behaviors can characterize feedback receptivity: *ignorance, rationalization,* or *acceptance.*

Ignorance is the result of information going in one ear and out the other. It is when we do not understand or hear what a person is telling us. I have participated in feedback sessions which resulted in a follow-up session. In that follow-up session, not only has the counseled executive's behavior not changed, but further, the executive denies ever having received the feedback in the first place!

In these instances, how do you get through? You will want the counseled executive to express to you *in writing* what he or she heard and how he or she plans to approach the needed improvement. The written documentation then becomes a strong deterrent to what I like to call "executive amnesia."

Feedback *rationalization* is a common reaction to undesirable or unwelcome feedback, particularly as you climb the organizational ladder. At this level, people are well-educated and creative but might be glib and fast on their feet. When critical feedback is delivered, they immediately go to work framing reasons for why the feedback is inaccurate or out of context. The best approach in dealing with a rationalizer is to *listen* to his or her rationale for believing that your observations are incorrect. After listening, summarize what you have heard and agree to continue to review his or her development needs as you go forward. Because the counseled executive has now explained to you what he or she believes you do not understand, the executive is obligated to respond to the "obvious misinterpretation" on your part. The executive has now heard you.

The last behavior is *acceptance* of feedback. This is an incredibly powerful behavior, which can accelerate your growth and improve your personal skill sets. As simple as accepting feedback may sound, it is not always that easy to do because we all have some level of ego. Our egos can be bruised easily by insensitively delivered feedback.

> Wise men speak because they have something to say;
> Fools because they have to say something.
> —Plato

Of course, if this is a book about how to achieve success and satisfaction, why am I spending time on these kinds of feedback behaviors? Because it is important to understand which behaviors to avoid and which to develop if you want to grow and prosper. Seldom can any of us achieve without coaching, support and feedback. The most often missed feedback is where people presume that you know the rules on how things work and yet you do not.

Understanding the heart of the company or organization of which you are a part is a powerful component of your personal growth trajectory. Every organization has its own DNA; that is, culture. It is based on a certain set of values, behaviors, dress codes and do's and don'ts that must be learned over time. Some are visible and observable. Others are easily shared in materials and conversation. Then there are those that are more subtle and must be experienced over time. It is important to understand exactly where you stand and how you fit in the DNA of the organization. It is particularly important for leaders. This comes from listening constructively to feedback.

Within many companies, there is a silent culture. An example; an organization can espouse values of being very expense conscious and a high value is placed on those that can cut costs and be inventive on cost control. But this same company might have an unspoken value that cost cutting should never be focused on the CEO's office and his staff. Why? Because the CEO believes that his organization already is "efficient" enough. This could be a reality that no one offers up to you, but you learn it from the stares of others, the body language of others, or from what others are not willing to discuss with you. These unspokens are hard to teach, so one must be sensitive and alert. This might not be the culture that is displayed to the world; it is larger and has much more influence on the inner workings of the people in the business. Often, workers don't see the silent culture until it's too late and they determine for themselves—or someone else determines for them—that they aren't fitting in. It is very important to listen at all times.

I recall attending a Wal-Mart Saturday Morning Meeting where the retired senior vice-chairman was the guest speaker. At that time, the first Saturday meeting of each month is referred to as "Culture Saturday," because management uses this forum to reinforce their people culture. Don Soderquist, made a particularly striking point about feedback. Don discussed the NASA 2003 Columbia disaster, in which all the astronauts were lost. He pointed out a negative aspect of NASA culture: specifically, "They did not want to bring negative feedback to the top." Apparently theirs was a culture that did not reward bad news, even when the bad news concerned the safety of NASA personnel and the overall program.

As a business leader it's your charge to communicate with the people in the organization, on their level, wherever they may be, instead of expecting others to communicate on yours. You must give them the feedback that is necessary for them to grow. That's the first step toward driving a simple business with real people at the core. Because costs are directly tied to retaining people, it is equally important to make sure that those you hire and develop are a good fit for both the job they are hired for and the culture at large. What if they are not? Face-to-face interviews and charisma sometimes get in the way of the truths revealed by a solid assessment tool or a personality-measurement test. It's important to establish a measuring system that is statistically proven to find the "perfect" fit—and listen when it finds that someone is the wrong fit. Sound too clinical? Feedback is very important, even before someone is hired.

After years in the HR arena, observing what people do to get ahead and the myriad of frustrations they face traveling a path to their goals, I can tell you that it's not easy to make good hiring decisions. The successful companies you consistently read about in business magazines focus on how to get, keep and grow their people; they have perfected the process of identifying, categorizing and integrating new hires. These organizations are as strategic about this as they are about the bottom line. They emphasize the need for receiving and listening to feedback from their employees.

The ear of the leader must ring with the voices of the people.
—Woodrow Wilson

Lesson 6

Develop Your People Skills

Let no one ever come to you without leaving better and
happier. Be the living expression of God's kindness:
kindness in your face, kindness in your eyes,
kindness in your smile.
—Mother Teresa

Probably one of the greatest barriers to success for many people is their lack of people skills. We can all tell stories of the rude treatment we received at the hands of a sales clerk, an airline ticket agent, or a municipal employee. We marvel at how they are able to keep their jobs while doling out punishment to those whom they serve or supervise. Few of these folks ever truly achieve success in their jobs. In many cases, if we were to follow their career histories, we would find that, if they have not been terminated altogether, their careers are stagnant.

Success in one's job and career requires several components. We already have outlined several of these components in the previous chapters. Job success also requires the ability to master the specific technical or professional skills in one's area. High levels of performance demonstrating the knowledge, skills, and abilities of a job are necessary for growth and development.

You might be familiar with the often-discussed bell-shaped performance curve. In business, the bell-curve view is that in any organization 15 percent of the employees are performing at an unsatisfactory level, 15 percent are performing above average, and 70 percent, the majority of the organization, are performing at an average level. While much debate can take place regarding the validity of this performance distribution, it does raise these questions: What separates our performance from that of others? Is it solely our successful execution of technical or professional skills? Or is there more?

We all have stories, not only about people who have treated us rudely, but about those people who stand out as pleasant to deal with, because they are honest, and hardworking. For example, I have had the same physician for many years. I learned that he was leaving his practice to become the head of administration at a regional hospital. It is a growing medical facility, which has undergone a major expansion of resources and services. It was no surprise that he would be asked to do more, particularly to serve in a role that had to do with managing others. Those who possess strong people skills can excel at their profession; but further, those skills increase the capacity to do more. Dr. Steven Goss always has been a fine, competent physician, who instilled confidence and clearly was a knowledgeable medical professional. What Dr. Goss exhibited, above and beyond those abilities that his patients expected, were strong human relations skills. In the medical field they call this great bedside manner! So, at the risk of embarrassing my friend and doctor, I believe that his people skills make him an exceptional physician and give him the capacity to do more.

The ability to deal effectively yet considerately with others can separate us from those who merely do the work. This people skill, the capacity to relate well to others, clearly is an element that can enhance performance. What are people skills and how do we acquire them? I do believe there are those who have natural abilities in this area, like other skills, but I also am convinced that good human relations skills can be learned and improved.

> Kind words can be short and easy to speak, but their echoes
> are truly endless.
> —Mother Theresa

I divide human relations skills into the three Cs: Connection, Consideration, and Communication.

Connection

Connection is the state of knowing that we each have something in common with one another. This "state of knowing" as I call it can be intuitive, or come from our own life's experiences. If we approach others and our environment with this expectation, we will be rewarded frequently. For example, there is a great likelihood that while traveling on a flight from Dallas to Chicago you will find something in common with the passenger next to you. Maybe you both live in Chicago, or you both were in Dallas on business, or you both love (or not love!) the Chicago Cubs. By connecting with one another around those things that we have in common, we form the basis of human relationships. This connectivity now separates that fellow passenger from a face in the crowd. As you deplane, he wishes you a good day or safe travels. Why? Because you now know that you have some shared experiences. This bonding, though quite brief, sets up a very human exchange that is an important part of establishing people skills—but this can only take place with the ability to communicate effectively.

Whether you realize it, you spend a lot more time listening than you do talking. During the listening process, it is important that you connect with the person to whom you are listening. If you don't connect, then you might start to daydream, or your thoughts could drift. For example, if you are an animal lover and someone in a discussion is using an example of how a puppy's innocent playfulness describes a situation, you are likely to work harder to pick up the relevance of the discussion because of your interest in pets. The communication has worked to spin up your receptivity by trying to find a connection to you.

To enhance your people skills, you must be able to connect with people, no matter what their level. The most successful communicators know how to do this and they do it very well. You can do the same thing.

If you want to lift yourself up, lift up someone else.
—Booker T. Washington

Communication

I do not propose to be an expert in this area, but I do know that we cannot connect with one another if we are not communicating! In the context of developing people skills, it is important that we are willing to give and receive information. As we discussed in chapter five, if we listen, we will learn a great deal. For instance, by listening we can learn what is important to others. By the same token, others get a sense of who we are.

Many take communication for granted because they think that communication is nothing more than talking, but there is much more to communication. Besides, you might say to yourself, I do it all the time. But if it is so easy, then how, when you say the same thing to two different people, can they interpret your words in different ways? This happens because we all process data differently. Because of this, it is possible to say one thing and find that the person you are addressing hears something completely different. It might be helpful to have that person repeat what you said. Summarizing a person's points in your own words reinforces the fact that 1) you were listening and 2) you understood accurately the person's point. This can clarify communication.

Why is communicating so important? It's important because we are always communicating, no matter what we do. If someone asks you a question and you don't say anything, you have communicated something to that person, even if you are not aware of it. Silence also can suggest resistance, uncertainty or anger, for example. We should be self-aware of what our silence could communicate to others. He or she either thinks that you are rude, hard of hearing, or just ignoring the question completely.

Body language also is another form of communicating. Although it is nonverbal communication, we still are sending messages to those around us. Body language can work in our favor or work against us. Our body language can signal to people that we want to either continue a conversation or move on to someone else. Emotions actually can show through our body language. That nonverbal communication can influence how people perceive our competence and receptiveness. Whatever we try to convey to others will show up in our body language. It starts in childhood and follows us all the way through life. The downside to body language is that it is sometimes misinterpreted. People can read your nonverbal cues the wrong way, so be conscious of this. Think about unintended messages you might be sending and work to restrain yourself from any potentially confusing body language.

We have to be especially careful when communicating through technology (e-mail, BlackBerries, text messages, and all social media) because, like silence and body language, it is so subjective.

You can write one thing and it can be interpreted differently. The absence of pitch, tonality and cadence easily can cause the reader to misinterpret what's written. Humor and sarcasm are particularly problematic for these reasons. Our world has become impersonal in many ways because we don't have to hear the human voice to carry on a conversation. Instant messaging and blogs have taken care of that.

Although you can't control what people say to you, you can control your reaction to it. The saying "Nobody can make you angry unless you let them," is very true. You determine what you will allow to "set you off." It doesn't matter what the person talking to you is communicating—what matters is the way you allow it to affect you.

> You can make more friends in two months by becoming
> really interested in other people than you can in two years
> by trying to get other people interested in you.
> —Dale Carnegie

Effective communication is a vital tool. Many terrible situations have occurred because of poor communication. We can see that from the shooting massacre at Virginia Tech in 2007. Seung-Hui Cho killed 32 people before turning the gun on himself. Had someone listened to his teachers and fellow classmates, when they told about the disturbing creative writing this young man had turned in, perhaps this could have been avoided. Cho was communicating. One might dare say he was even crying out for help, but those around him were unable to communicate on his level. Failure to communicate, as we saw, can lead to disaster. That is not to say it was the teachers, classmates, or anyone's fault, it simply was more of a miscommunication. We constantly communicate to others; it is just a matter of whether we are effective. Communication easily can be misunderstood. In many cases, marriages end, customers decide never to return to establishments, employees quit their jobs, and even wars are waged because of deficient communication skills. Make sure that your mind is engaged before you open your mouth to convey a thought! Also, if you are the listener, be sure to seek clarity and understanding. Both speaking and listening take work!

Consideration

Consideration is a behavioral style that expresses caring and concern for another. When you talk, others really don't care how much you know until they know how much you care. This consideration comes across in the way that we talk to others, through our tone of voice and our demeanor.

It is vital that once you hear information from another individual you process it to make sure you correctly heard what the person said. Once you have heard it, not just with your ears but with your heart, then you are in a position to consider what was said. We all have been in conversations in which we were aware that the persons to whom we were talking were not considering what we were saying because they were too preoccupied with what they would say next.

You probably have been told throughout your life to be considerate of others. When you work on your people skills, this is of the utmost importance. By doing all the talking, you are having a one-way conversation. Is that really effective communication? Who benefits from this type of communication? This is why consideration is so important. You want to be heard, but you also want to make sure that you are being understood. If you don't know or care whether the person understands you, you are lacking consideration. Consideration and communication really go hand in hand.

For example, have you ever seen a parent reprimanding a teenager, and the parent goes on and on and on, and the child never gets to say a word? More than likely, you can tell from the child's face that he or she is not listening, but is staring into space. This is not good communication. At best, the parent is talking to himself or herself.

It's no different in the corporate world. You know those long, drawn-out meetings with a speaker up front, going from one topic to the next, and never giving the audience a chance to say anything. After a while, participants' thoughts begin to wander. Some think about the project they need to get done, what they are going to eat for lunch, or how they are going to get help with all that work stacked on their desk. Consideration is necessary.

Even in a one-on-one meeting between an employee and employer, consideration is vital if progress is to be made. If the employer does all of the talking and never gives the employee the opportunity to express his or her opinion or thoughts, then consideration is not taking place. It is a one-sided conversation. Once you know that you and the person you are talking with have made a mental connection, you are moving into the realm of a meaningful conversation and true communication is taking place. Success comes along with developing good communication, and good people skills come along with being kind to others on your way to the top.

They may forget what you said, but they will never forget
how you made them feel.
—Carl W. Buechner (Author)

Lesson 7

Have Humility

Humility is to make a right estimate of one's self.
—Charles H. Spurgeon

Pat Summitt, the Hall of Fame women's basketball coach at the University of Tennessee, and at the time of this writing, the winningest coach in NCAA history, is a well-known and well-recognized personality. In the off-season, she does extensive speaking around the United States and shares an interesting story. Pat reports that she was out at lunch with a friend one day, at a very nice restaurant, when she noticed that the women at the next table were staring at her. They pointed at her and nodded their heads knowingly. Of course, as she explains, Pat was somewhat used to being recognized around town and the country, so she simply smiled politely. About halfway through her lunch, one of the women approached her, and said, "You can tell that we were discussing you at our table. Aren't you the woman that works at the local Home Depot?"

I have had similar experiences. As the executive vice president of the People Division (human resources) of Wal-Mart Stores Inc., I had human resources responsibility; which consisted of ensuring that we were recruiting capable people to perform the many functions of our company, retaining good people through good leadership, pay and benefits and providing people the opportunity to grow their careers, for more than one million associates in the United States and another 500,000 in our international operations. In that role, I frequently traveled around the United States and internationally, visiting our stores and offices. Also, because of our own Wal-Mart television network and newspaper distribution, I was a fairly well-recognized person in the company. It was not unusual for me to encounter Wal-Mart people wherever I traveled, particularly in airports and on airplanes.

One evening I was returning home through the Dallas\Fort Worth airport. While waiting in the terminal, I noticed a man and woman smiling and nodding at me from several rows over. I smiled back politely and assumed that they were company employees and were excited to know that one of their high-ranking executives was going to be on the same airplane with them. As the airline personnel called us to begin boarding, the couple approached me and asked, "Are you Cole Peterson?" With puffed-up false modesty, I replied, yes, prepared to receive comments on how nice it was to meet a senior officer of the company. Rather, the woman exclaimed to her husband, "See, I told you, this is Shirley Peterson's husband—we think your wife is wonderful! She has helped our family and our children in ways that we cannot thank her enough. Be sure to tell her that we said hello and thanks so much for all she has done!" My wife, Shirley, whom most people know as "Peaches," worked for a number of years as a scholarship counselor in our local high school. In that role, she has touched the lives of many young people, steering them to the best fit colleges and universities, as well as helping them to secure scholarship monies and financial aid.

After I recovered from my deflated ego, I thanked them for being so appreciative and promised that I would carry their message of gratitude home to Peaches. I chuckled to myself on the entire flight home thinking, "Now here is a great lesson: have humility; it is not about you."

What is your story? Is it about you? Do you have humility or nothing more than false modesty? This lesson has such power because much of our own ability to grow through establishing relationships with others has to do with our ability to keep our egos in check.

To be fair, most successful and upwardly mobile people have a healthy dose of ego. After all, if we were not self-confident, how would we project our skills and abilities to others? No one wants to follow an insecure, self-doubting leader. At the same time, humility draws the best of others to us.

> Humility makes great men twice honorable.
> —Benjamin Franklin

In the Super Bowl of 2007, much was made of the fact that two African-American coaches were squaring off against each other: Lovie Smith of the Chicago Bears and Tony Dungy of the Indianapolis Colts. Each coach played down the significance of this event (although it was truly historic) to focus on the players and appreciation of the support from the Chicago and Indianapolis fans. What was particularly striking to the world was the amazing humility in the leadership styles of both men. At this juncture in their careers, when they had certainly earned the right to high-five each other and expound on their greatness, they assumed a much more reserved attitude. All of us take cues from the leader. The behavior of these two coaches telegraphed some very positive characteristics to their teams (and we often forget how young and impressionable many of our professional athletes are today!). It telegraphed mutual respect. It telegraphed a maturity that demonstrated that it is never "all about me" or about one person. It is about the team.

I submit that there is a high correlation between success and those who have the ability to keep themselves and their egos in check. We all want to be somebody and leave an impact on the world. We want to know that we matter and that we make a difference just by being alive. We want to be significant. There are those who are simply self-serving and those on the other end of the pendulum who are self-sacrificing. Humility is somewhere between those two extremes.

Because we live in such a competitive society, is it even possible to practice humility? On a daily basis, you might hear someone saying, "You have got to put in extra hours if you want to make it to the top!" This type of mentality pushes us to boast when we reach the next rung or achieve the next goal or receive the next promotion. Therefore, how does one go about having humility?

When we hear the word humility, we usually hear the word meek, and when we hear the word meek, we usually think of the word weak. It is indeed a good thing to be humble, but discovering how to achieve it can be elusive because the world in which we live is so focused on being a winner. You will notice that, from sports to business and everything in between, the goal is to be a winner. Then, once the winner is selected, humility usually goes out the window. Most will find it easy to be around those who are humble, but when it comes to humbling ourselves it is quite a different story. Some might even say that being too humble can stand in the way of success.

Success and humility go together. Most of those who are successful have a competitive spirit and are very ambitious. That is not a bad thing, but channeling that spirit and ambition in the right way and keeping the right frame of mind is where the work comes in. It is very natural and normal to feel proud when a goal has been reached or an accomplishment achieved, but exaggerated pride is the opposite of humility. It is very easy to look around and see that there is no shortage of people in the world that have over-the-top pride. Humility is a choice.

Humility is the foundation of all the other virtues.
—Saint Augustine

Simon Cowell, of *American Idol* fame, provides us with a great example of humility. When Jennifer Hudson was a contestant on the show, he proclaimed that she was out of her league and that she would never succeed. The American public voted her off the show the same week. However, after her incredible success in the 2006 blockbuster movie, *Dreamgirls*, he apologized for his previous estimation of her. After seeing Hudson perform on *The Oprah Winfrey Show*, Cowell was forced to admit his mistake, saying "I would like to be the first to admit a massive dose of humble pie. Because there are good performances and occasionally there are extraordinary performances. That was extraordinary, Jennifer, and I feel very proud for you."[7] As someone renowned more for his inclination to give criticism than to give praise, Cowell displayed a lot of humility in this situation.

Many people believe that those who are full of pride always finish first. Tony Dungy, the coach of the Indianapolis Colts, displayed an amazing sense of humility upon winning Super Bowl XLI. He stated, "I'm proud to be the first African-American coach to win this. But again, more than anything, Lovie Smith and I are not only African American but Christian coaches, showing you can do it the Lord's way. We're more proud of that." He could have taken all of the glory for himself and talked about his strategy, his game plans, or his players, but he gave the honor to God—that took humility.

> There is no limit to what you can accomplish if you don't
> care who gets the credit.
> —Ronald Reagan

You might be wondering: Haven't you heard the saying, "Take pride in your work or whatever you do"? Well, how can you be humble and take pride in your work at the same time? It sounds like an oxymoron.

I believe that there is a healthy balance in there somewhere. A dose of humility is what it takes to get to the top of the ladder in any profession or area of life. A person who has humility possesses inner strength as well as confidence. A humble person wants to do the right thing. They are not bent on doing things their way, because they are aware that their way is not always the best way. Those with humility welcome constructive criticism because they realize it is a way to improve. They are not afraid of change because change is a part of growth and improvement. It has been said that the person who is truly humble will not be defensive when others confront them about an idea. He or she knows that working on a weakness is a true sign of strength.

It is possible to be humble and assertive at the same time. A humble person will be more likely to admit a fault quickly, yet he or she will also take a compliment in the right perspective. He or she knows just the right words to say when accepting praise.

Humility is a great character trait; it helps to keep the ego in check and allows us to be more productive. Pride, as the saying goes, "cometh before the fall." Many prideful people think that they don't need anyone because they are convinced of their own superiority. It's not hard to see that such a person is headed for a fall. The best leaders are the ones who are humble enough to be taught and those they will supervise will not mind being taught by them. Let's avoid the personality of the character in the song "It's Hard to Be Humble," by Mac Davis: "Oh Lord, it's hard to be humble / when you're perfect in every way, / I can't wait to look in the mirror / 'cause I get better lookin' each day. / To know me is to love me, / I must be a hell of a man. / Oh Lord, it's hard to be humble, / but I'm doin' the best that I can."[8] While this is fun and amusing, it is not who we want to be!

Rather than having such pride, let's assume the attitude of Gandhi.

> I claim to be a simple individual, liable to err like any other fellow mortal. I own, however, that I have humility enough to confess my errors and to retrace my steps.
> —Mahatma Gandhi

Lesson 8

Get a Life

And in the end, it's not the years in your life that count.
It's the life in your years.
—Abraham Lincoln

As my daughter was growing up, one of her favorite sayings was, "Get a life!" She would respond with this whenever I teased her about getting something done a certain way or when I offered my opinion about some of her teenage antics and behaviors. But, from the mouths of babes can come true wisdom.

For so many of us, it is true that we need to get a life. We've all heard the statement that when we are on our death bed, none of us will wish that we had spent more time at the office. This oft-recounted statement touches us at our most basic level: What is life really about? Am I finding joy? If I were to die tomorrow, would I feel today that I had lived a full life?

We live in a competitive society, so we know it is important to come out of the starting blocks fast and hard. We want to provide for our families and enjoy the comforts that money and success can provide. As a result, we set our priorities early in life; one of which is to work hard. As the successes come, we require a bigger paycheck, a bigger office, and a bigger house.

To be clear: there is certainly nothing wrong with succeeding and enjoying the fruits of our labors. During graduate school, I completed my thesis on a topic called "Middleessence." *Middleessence* is the study and the way of living, of midlife (roughly 50 to 60 years of age.) One day, I was struck by an article about a high-powered Wall Street type who retired suddenly and moved to the South Pacific to become a painter. I was fascinated with the developments that led him to the decision. His view was simple. He was successful in the financial sense, but had never really self-actualized; that is, he had never become all that he could have become. He decided that, before it was too late, he wanted to explore other aspects of life.

> We make a living by what we get,
> but we make a life by what we give.
> —Winston Churchill

Now, I am not proposing that we all check out of our jobs and head for Tahiti. Our challenge is to ensure that we have a healthy balance between work, family, and self. My experience has led me to detect an interesting behavior regarding this balance. The hardworking individual strives so hard for that upward mobility, that next promotion, that he or she begins identifying more with a job title than with family and self. Therefore, my advice to all is: understand that *your job is not you!*

Over the years, I have observed individuals who identify with and, at all costs, protect the titles on their business cards. I have noticed many employees, supervisors, and executives who have worked for years in jobs in which they were miserable because the outside world had a high regard for the company for which they worked, or because they had attained an impressive job title.

71

Certainly we all know that we must be gainfully employed. It is also prudent to give 110 percent to our jobs and responsibilities. At the same time, when we get to a place where we have no identity without our job, we have lost ourselves.

I decided, as a result of my middlessence project in graduate school, to set my own personal objectives early. Because I came from very humble beginnings, I always reminded myself that I would never need to compromise myself because I could always go back to driving a taxicab (which I did during my latter years in college). In the years immediately after I finished college, being unmarried allowed me to throw myself into my work without much consideration for other aspects of my life. After all, as a single guy in my 20s, I did not need to plan much to call my buddies and have them meet me for a beer! However, as life moved on and I married my wonderful wife, I learned to carefully consider the balance between work and life.

> We are always getting ready to live but never living.
> —Ralph Waldo Emerson

As many of us know, the real challenge comes along with having children and raising your family. Raising our children is the most rewarding, and sometimes the most demanding, job in our lives. Because this is so, we run the risk of missing some of the most meaningful times in both our own and our children's lives.

I have always told my family and friends that I want to be like that American Express commercial that showed the dad who traveled home from wherever he was in the world to be at his children's special events. Today, I hope that my children would say that their dad was there for the piano recitals, dance performances, swim meets, and basketball games. The parents working to accomplish this, in doing so, find tremendous relaxation and satisfaction, which can affect the pressures and stresses of our jobs.

Some of you may say, "Well, Coleman, it was easy for you to be such a stellar dad, because you were a senior executive, with access to company planes and control of your own schedule!" Not so. As many of us have learned, the higher up the corporate or organizational ladder you go, the more requirements and responsibilities are placed on you.

The commitment to balance in life is a personal one that forces each of us to decide how we want to spend our time. For example, when my daughter was seven years old, she was a member of our neighborhood swim team. I enjoyed attending those swim meets, which generally occurred on weekdays, in the late afternoon and evening. I was struck by the fact that the same parents always attended the meets. There were several families whose members worked for the same company as I did, so I was familiar with workloads and company requirements, yet I never saw certain members of those families at the meets. I always wondered whether they had a second job, had elected to work late, or simply had something more important to do. Life choices! We can never know what another person's situations are in life, but we each make our own choices.

While discussing this topic with a group some time ago, I was asked if I was being unrealistic about my "supermom" or "superdad" philosophy. After all, can we really be expected to attend all of the events in our children's and family's lives and still successfully provide for our families? I believe that, yes, we can be expected to attend events in our children's lives and still provide. Certainly not all events. I have found our families are reasonable. Early on, I felt guilty when I was unable to attend one of my children's activities. Then, in discussion with them, I learned that they really did not expect me to be there all of the time. *They just wanted to know that I wanted to be there and that I would be there whenever I could!* This reaction comes from establishing early, positive relationships with our children, sharing time and experiences. When we build on the knowledge that family time is important, our children will not question our interest in their lives.

> Twenty years from now, you will be more disappointed
> by the things you didn't do than by the ones you did do.
> So throw off the bowlines. Sail away from the safe harbor.
> Catch the trade winds in your sails.
> Explore. Dream. Discover.
> —Mark Twain

One habit that my wife and I adopted was to sit down at the beginning of each year with a calendar and pencil in the major school and extracurricular activities that would take place during the year. Then we would add other family events like reunions, weddings, and so on. We would compare this against important activities at our jobs, such as annual meetings, special presentations, and travel. With this information we could determine the best times to take vacations and personal time. This even enabled us to talk to our supervisors well in advance if special time off was going to be needed.

Oftentimes we say that we cannot do a certain thing because "My boss won't let me get away," or "My schedule won't allow it," when in fact we have not made sufficient plans. What is important enough in your life to plan ahead for? As you look back on a year at its close, are you satisfied that you sufficiently advanced your career as well as your personal well-being? Remember, life is not just the destination; it's the journey!

If you truly want to be happy with your job and yourself, then you need to start enjoying your life outside of the job. Jobs come and go, but your life outside of work will always be there. Success on the job is actually made sweeter when you can share it with your family and those that you love. Like the saying goes, "All work and no play makes Jack a dull boy." It's true. If you spend all of your time working, what are you going to do when you are no longer employed and you have lost your family along the way?

> We Americans are living a lifestyle of exhaustion.
> We don't have time for ourselves, much less
> for each other and our children.
> —James Dobson, Ph.D.

I submit that those who are unhappy in their personal lives are, for the most part, the same people who are unhappy in their jobs. Why is that? Your job is only part of your life, not your entire life. It is great to be successful, but success should not come at the expense of closing those you love out of your life.

If you are looking to your job as your "real" life, you may not find joy and satisfaction there. The real meaning in your life is likely to come outside of the office. Simply stated, to find meaning in one's life away from your work, ensure that your work reinforces, rather than negatively affects, life away from work. A job is the means by which you support yourself financially. Therefore, it is imperative that you find one that you truly enjoy. Make sure you look for a position that uses your skills and abilities, people who have a healthy respect for you and your life outside of the job, a company with integrity, and a job that makes you want to get up and go there every day. Those who enjoy their jobs tend to be happier at home and in every area of their lives.

The best balance to have in your life is one that gives you purpose at home and on the job. It is very possible to have the best of both worlds, but you have to set the necessary boundaries to achieve it. All you have to do is look at a workaholic to see that something is badly out of balance. If you were to speak to the family of a workaholic, you would find that this imbalance affects the individual's family as well; they would immediately be able to list the out of balance elements in their life.

A balance between professional life and personal life is like a key lime pie. Your job is like the other ingredients in the filling of the pie. When you mix those two together, you can have a great dessert—and a great life. However, when you separate them, they are not as flavorful. After all, by themselves, limes are sour.

> People, even more than things, have to be restored,
> renewed, revived, reclaimed, and redeemed;
> never throw out anyone.
> —Audrey Hepburn

It's very important that you know yourself. Know your limitations. Know what makes you happy. Know what brings you true joy. Yes, you will find pleasure in a job and in other people, but you still need to get to the things that make you truly happy. It could be something as simple as going to the park with friends or family. No matter what it is, you need to find it.

Your job is indeed part of you, but it is not the totality of your being. It does influence every part of your life. Work is vital to your existence, but what you do in the other parts of your life is equally vital. You must be able to see beyond the job.

As you age and mature, you will begin to see the different dimensions of your life and go in the direction of those permanent parts of life, such as your family. Relationships will last; jobs will come and jobs will go. Once you get over this hurdle, realizing that your job is not who you are, then you are free to take risks that you would not have taken otherwise. If you remain defined by your job, at some point you are going to have to let that go. Because life is worth living, embrace it and live it to the fullest. By doing so, you will find pleasure in your job and in your life.

Many people die with their music still in them. Why is this so? Too often it is because they are always getting ready to live. Before they know it, time runs out.
—Oliver Wendell Holmes

Lesson 9

Help Somebody

Everybody can be great, because everybody can serve.
—Dr. Martin Luther King, Jr.

My most influential heroes are Mother Teresa, Mohandas K. Gandhi, and Dr. Martin Luther King, Jr. I know that I could never measure up to the degree of selflessness and giving that each displayed—even unto death.

Mother Teresa's given name was Agnes Gonxha Bojaxhiu. When she was only 12 years old, she strongly felt the call of God in her life and desired to be a missionary. She left home at age 18 to become a nun. After her training, she was sent to Calcutta, India. She taught school for a while, but she was so moved by the poverty within the city that she requested permission to work among the poor within the land. She depended totally upon God to fund her mission, including the school that she opened for the children in the slums of Calcutta. Mother Teresa went from house to house, visiting families. It was not uncommon for her to wash the sores of children. She once took care of an old man, lying sick on the road, and she was known for nursing a woman dying of hunger and tuberculosis. Near the end of her life, Mother Teresa experienced severe health problems, yet she still continued to minister to the needs of the poor. Her testimony is one of strong faith, strong hope, and unbelievable charity—that is, helping others.

> We can do no great things, only small things with great love.
> —Mother Teresa

Mahatma Gandhi's given name was Mohandas Karamchand Gandhi and he was born in Porbandar, India. He was one of the most respected spiritual and political leaders of the 1900s. When he tried to claim his right as a British citizen, he was abused. As a result of this abuse, Gandhi was able to understand the suffering of all Indians[9].

Gandhi was arrested several times by the British because of his activities in South Africa and India. As long as it was for a just cause, he felt it was admirable to go to jail. He actually spent seven years in prison for his political activities. He developed a plan of action that was based upon courage, nonviolence, and truth. He promoted nonviolence and civil disobedience as the best methods for achieving political and social goals. He also believed in fasting as a way to impress the use of nonviolence upon others. He was very instrumental in helping to free the Indian people through nonviolent resistance of British rule. He believed in helping others, regardless of the personal cost. As we know, Gandhi's nonviolent philosophy was adopted by Dr. Martin Luther King, Jr. in the pursuit of civil rights in the United States.

> You must be the change you wish to see in the world.
> —Gandhi

Martin Luther King, Jr. was born Michael Luther King in Atlanta, Georgia. Around 6 years old, his first name was changed to match his dad's. One of his first acts as part of the civil rights movement was when he assembled the black community during a 382-day boycott of Montgomery Alabama bus lines. He was arrested, suffered violent harassment and the bombing of his house, but he never gave up. He spent the majority of his life fighting discrimination. He was a leader of the civil-rights movement in America from the mid-1950s until he was assassinated in Memphis, Tennessee in 1968[10].

Dr. King preached nonviolence to achieve civil rights reform. He led a mass protest in Birmingham regarding fair hiring practices and the desegregation of department-store facilities. He was once again arrested, but he didn't keep silent. He wrote his famous *Letters from a Birmingham Jail* during that time. On another occasion, in Selma, Alabama, he led a voter-registration campaign that ended in the famous Selma-to-Montgomery freedom march. He even took his crusade to Chicago. There, he launched programs to renovate slums and provide housing for blacks. He gave his all, even his very life, to help others. It was said that when he died, at the age of 39, that his heart was in the condition of a 60- or 70-year-old person. He lived and helped others with passion.

Life's most urgent question is: What are you doing for others?
—Dr. Martin Luther King, Jr.

The great message for you and me is: We need not try to equal the sacrifice of the truly great. Our challenge is to simply make a difference in our small part of the world.

I am convinced that most of us underestimate our influence on others and the impact we have on others.

Coleman,

I hope you remember me! My name was Laura Vogler way back in the early 1980's. I was your Administrative Assistant when you relocated from Chicago to St. Louis as the Director of Training & Development for Venture Stores. We worked together for several years, then I moved to the warehouse facility in O'Fallon to work for Darlene Elder as her assistant HR manager. From there I moved into several stores as the HR manager. I left Venture in 1988 when I accepted a position with McDonnell Douglas, now Boeing. I spent eleven years in the Finance organization and began to miss the HR world. I went back to school to earn my Master's in HRM which allowed me to move into an HR generalist position. I worked as a generalist supporting several military programs and was promoted into HR management. I currently support the Engineering division in St. Louis and St. Charles. My team of six generalists and I support approximately 6,000 engineers!

The reason I'm writing is to let you know the impact you had on my professional life back then and still today. You were my first mentor and the advice and counsel you gave me back then still has an impact on me today. My administrative assistant recently completed her Bachelor's degree and is hoping to move into a generalist position. The same sage words of advice you gave me I passed on to her. I spoke so highly of you to her she asked if I had a

*picture. I did an internet search and found your Hollis
Enterprises website. You look terrific by the way!*

*Coleman, I want you to know that I will always be
grateful to you for helping a young college grad find a path
to a very rewarding and satisfying career AND enabling
me to pass it on to others as I help them find their way!*

Laura Park
August 5, 2010

When I received this wonderful letter, I realized that Laura
may have thought that I had no idea what an impact our meeting
had on her life; however, as I reflected on it, I did understand it.
I understood it because of the impact that others have had on
my life. Helping somebody need not be some grandiose act, yet
it can sometimes produce amazing results. Here is an incredibly
touching letter sent to me by the son of a former work associate.

Mr. Peterson,

*I am sure that you don't remember me, but I am the
son of Tom Gent that worked with you at Venture Stores.
It has been a long time since he passed away and I wasn't
old enough at the time to understand the respect that my
father had for you as a college and individual. Now that
I am older and have been in the work force for several
years, I have come to understand that the most significant
accomplishment one can make is his/her career is building
the respect and trust of those that work around them. My
father was not the type of person to say a bad thing about
anybody, but I could always tell when he talked about*

somebody how he felt about them. It was always very apparent to me that when he spoke about you that he had a lot of respect and admiration for you.

A few weeks ago a former customer of mine told one of my colleges that I made a significant difference in his life by talking to him on the importance of taking his vacation time and spending it with his family. Up until that time, he never took much vacation and they never had a family trip. After our conversation, he took his first family trip and to this day credits me for making him see what was important. It felt pretty good to get that message and it got me thinking that I should pass on what my father thought of you. My father didn't talk about a lot of people from work, but you were one of the few. I want to thank you for making a difference in his life and making his day at work more pleasurable as he truly enjoyed working with you.

Take care,
Allen Gent

Do you remember the Liberty Mutual insurance commercial in which one individual's act of kindness encourages another to do the same? One person helps another when he falls in the street; that man then holds an elevator door for a woman in a hurry; a witness to this act then stops a delivery truck from backing into a motorcycle; a woman witnesses this event and later stops a coworker from falling over in his chair. This chain reaction of helpful behavior continues throughout the commercial.

Shortly after I noted this remarkable commercial, there was a string of such events in New York City that were especially newsworthy. The first was of a man who jumped onto the train tracks in the New York subway to save a man who had fallen there. The second was a pair of NYC policemen who delivered a baby on the subway, and the third was several men who, while walking down a New York street, became aware of a child who had climbed out on a windowsill several stories up. Together, they were able to catch the child before he hit the ground!

> The more I help others to succeed, the more I succeed.
> —Ray Kroc

One other incidence of people reaching out to help someone occurred in March 2007, in the Bronx, New York, when a fire broke out in a house where seventeen people were living. Neighbors and friends came running to assist these families in whatever way they could. As a mother threw her children from the burning building, neighbors, friends, and firemen caught them. They even caught her when she jumped from the building. This is mankind at its best—helping someone.

These are pretty dramatic events that underscore the bravery and caring of one person for another. Yet it is simply being who we are and being tuned into others that presents us with the opportunity to help others. Probably the most impactful story that has come to me was through a Wal-Mart Stores customer-service letter. A customer wrote this letter to "Whom It May Concern."

"I wanted to write and share with you how one of your cashiers literally saved my life. I stayed in Mena for a few months with my sister while I battled severe depression. I was going through a divorce after twenty years of marriage and had never lived alone. I was scared and devastated. One night last November, I decided to give up and kill myself. I went into your store and bought three bottles of (fifty count) over the counter sleeping pills and had intended to take all of them! I got in line to pay for them, planning where I would go park my car, take the pills and die. While waiting in line, I witnessed an act of sheer compassion. An elderly lady, while paying for her purchases began to cry. The cashier came out from behind the counter and held the little old lady. I could only hear part of the conversation. The woman had recently lost her husband, they had been married almost sixty years and even shopping without him was rather painful for her. The cashier, whose name is Carly, comforted this woman. I could tell by the conversation that they did not even know one another! When it became my turn, Carly asked how I was doing. I replied that I was doing okay. She looked right into my eyes and asked if I was sure about that. She told me later that she could tell that I was hurting. I never confided that I had every intention on ending it all that night. She confided in me her own secrets of getting through tough times. She said that it is important to laugh every single day. She then told me some very funny and clean jokes. I was so impressed that a cashier at Wal-Mart took the time to care about a stranger. She told me several things that have helped me so much. At night, when I'm alone and I begin to fall apart, I put into practice the things she shared with me. One of the things I do is rent funny movies. I laugh, even when I would rather cry. I do not know if you have any idea that you have a very special person working for you, but you do!! Thank you, Wal-Mart and THANK YOU Carly. Because of you, I'm alive. Laughter is really a medicine.

May God bless every Wal-Mart with at least one Carly. Thank you for the rest of my precious life, Tina Warren."

Our responsibility as citizens of the world is to leave it somewhat better than how we found it when we came—we should make a difference.

> To do more for the world than the world
> does for you—that is success.
> —Henry Ford

Lesson 10

Be Thankful

Be thankful for what you have; you'll end up having more.
If you concentrate on what you don't have, you will never,
ever have enough.
—Oprah Winfrey

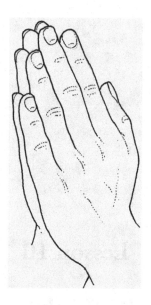

At this late stage, I can confess to you that I really did not want to write this book for several reasons. For example, who would really want to read my book? Exactly what value do I have to offer? Additionally, as I have found, writing a book is hard work. It requires conscientious attention to the subject matter to be sure the reader is able to make sense of the writer's experiences. My experiences are initially clear to only me. The challenge of unraveling all of one's thoughts and experiences, then relating them in a way to make it meaningful for others is a critical part of writing, yet it is exhausting.

On my retirement from Wal-Mart, I had visions of playing two rounds of golf daily, punctuated by an occasional margarita and a nicely rolled cigar. I received frequent questions about when I planned to write a book. At that point, the thought had not occurred to me. However, after several discussions about this idea, I decided that I would spend some time working on a book. I spent several months working, on material for several chapters, only to determine that I did not like much of what I had done. I did not like the material because it was too clinical and "textbookish," which is not what I wanted to convey. So I walked away from the material and felt unable to get going again.

I considered scrapping the entire project, until I began hearing from others, who were disappointed that I had not made much progress. They were very reinforcing and insisted that I had some important things to share. Freda Dents, a collaborator with me on this book, was most persuasive on this topic. She explained that I underestimated what I had accomplished; for many men and women who are seeking their own paths to success, what I have to share is of real value to them. My reply was "Yes, and I thank God for my good fortune."

> When I started counting my blessings,
> my whole life turned around.
> —Willie Nelson

That was the point of inspiration for me. If I am able to share any lessons that may be helpful in others' lives, then this has been a worthwhile engagement. Therefore, I would be remiss if I did not share my belief that in addition to our free will that allows us to learn skills and gain experiences that advance our careers, I believe that there is a Higher Power that blesses and guides our events.

The very idea that an inner-city kid could rise from the housing projects of Chicago to the executive level of the No. 1 company in *Fortune* magazine's top 500 companies is a great story. But the story is not just in the telling; the story is in understanding that what drives us and motivates us to accomplish our goals is *faith*: faith in the belief that man is basically good and that our Creator wanted us to do well and succeed in this life as well as the next.

Your spiritual belief can and will have a tremendous impact on how you move forward in life. Do you move forward with pessimism or optimism? Do you believe that you have a right to joy in this life, or is this world a veil of tears for you?

I once was asked about whether the global expansion plans of Wal-Mart would be successful because of Wal-Mart's strong culture. Would that strong culture translate to other workforces around the world? I have often shared my response to that question; that is, there are such things as universal truths.

Universal truths are, to me, values that transcend geography, religion, race, gender, economic status, and politics. They are those truisms that we all respond to. How can company cultures translate around the world? By addressing universal truths, we can succeed. For example:

What person in the world would not want to be successful at his or her job?

What person would not want to work for a great boss?

What person would not want to be judged on the quality of his or her work (rather than race, gender, religion, etc.)?

What person would not want to work in a safe, clean environment?

As you can see, I could go on for a quite a while, detailing these things on which we universally agree. I believe that God dwells there. We each have a spiritual center. To what degree it is developed is a result of our own upbringing and training. I would say, to each of you who have read this far, believe in yourself, believe in others and believe that there is a Higher Power that guides us, which can energize and lift us up.

How often do you thank God for the things that He has done in your life? We don't want to be like the 10 lepers (Luke 17:11-19). The Bible reports that on his journey to Jerusalem,

Jesus encountered 10 lepers who pleaded with him to heal them. Jesus directed them to their priests and as they were on their way, the Bible reports that they all were healed. Only one of them, when he realized that he was healed, returned to thank Jesus. Only one of the 10 returned. I hope that our percentages are much better than that!

When a person doesn't have gratitude, something is missing
in his or her humanity. A person can almost be defined
by his or her attitude toward gratitude.
—Elie Wiesel (Author, Nobel Peace Prize Winner)

In America, we celebrate the holiday of Thanksgiving once a year, but we should always be thankful. Nearly every religious culture of the world has a time of Thanksgiving, whether it is Hanukah in the Jewish culture, Ramadan in the Muslim faith, or Kwanzaa in the African-American culture to cite a few. If you look at your life, you will find so many things to be thankful for. If you are reading this, then you are still alive, and that gives you something to be thankful for. I can honestly say that I have been blessed beyond measure. I had no idea that I would have made it to this point in my life, but the journey has been great.

When you do a good deed for someone, one of the things that can bring such joy to your heart is for them to say two words: "Thank you." God is no different. He wants us to be thankful for the many blessings that he has given to us. It delights him when we let him know that we are grateful. I have learned, through the years, that all of my blessings flow from him.

Never take for granted the things that you have been given, because at any moment they can be taken away. One day, people were in their homes enjoying life; the next day, they were standing on the top of houses calling for someone to lift them up out of the waters in New Orleans, Louisiana. One day, students were sitting in a classroom being instructed by a professor; the next day, their lives were shattered when a fellow student randomly killed 32 people. Life can change in a moment.

Learn to be thankful for all things. Both joy and sorrows serve a purpose in our lives. We don't always know these purposes, but they reveal themselves over time. We will either become bitter or better.

The results of being thankful are numerous. Your fears will leave, your complaints will disappear, and your worries will dissipate. Most of all, God will be glorified! You will also receive joy, the peace of God, and courage. The more thankful you are, the more blessings you will receive. Because we want blessings to keep flowing our way, we don't ever want to stop giving thanks.

God has given me innumerable blessings; I could not begin to recount them. Thank you for taking this journey with me. I'm so thankful to God and you.

Endnotes

1   Belkin, Doulas. "Struggling for recruits Army relaxed its rules". Boston Globe, February 20, 2006, news section, nation.

2   TaipeiTimes.com, "Letter: Keep UN out of languages". http:// taipeitimes.com/news/editorials/archives/2007/05/24/2003362262

3   About.com: US government Info, "US Graduation Rate Hits All Time High". http://usgovinfo.about.com/od/censusandstatistics/a/ highschool.htm.

4   UNGEI.org, "'Will You Listen? Young voices from conflict zones?" (2007). http://www.ungei.org/resources/1612_1582.html.

5   ABC News, "John Stossel's Stupid in America—How lack of choice cheats our kids out of a good education". http://abcnes. go.com/2020/stossel/story?id+1500338

6   ABC News, "John Stossel's Stupid in America—How lack of choice cheats our kids out of a good education". http://abcnes. go.com/2020/stossel/story?id+1500338

7   Oprah.com, "The Stars of Dreamgirls". www.oprah.com/tows/ slide/200611/20061120/slide_20061120_350_109.jhtmml.

8   www.lyricsmode.com, "It's Hard To Be Humble lyrics by Mac Davis'. http://www.lyricsmode.com/lyrics/m/mac_davis/its_hard_to_be_humble.html.

9   Wikkipedia.com, "Mohandas Karamchand Gandhi". http:// en.wikipedia.org/wiki/Mahatma_Gandhi.

10 Wikipedia.com, "Martin Luther King, Jr." http://en.wikipedia. org/wiki/Martin_Luther_King